Shortcut to Swedish:

Beginner's Guide to Quickly Learning the Basics of the Swedish Language

ANNIKA SVENSSON

WOLFEDALE PRESS

Cover image by: Tommaso Lizzul

ISBN: 978-0995930506

CONTENTS

INTRODUCTION:
HOW TO LEARN SWEDISH

SETTING GOALS

Learning a new language is seen by many, especially English speakers, as an extremely complicated, time-consuming task and one that above a certain age is not really practical, or even possible, anymore. Learning a new language can indeed be a lot of work, but it is nowhere near impossible; in fact in many societies around the world it is the norm to speak more than one language, and sometimes several. As an English speaker you probably don't feel that you need to speak any other language and for the most part that is true. But despite this, you want to learn a new language, or are at least considering it, or you wouldn't be reading this. Learning a new language can be an extremely enriching experience and one that I feel everyone should at least honestly attempt.

What I encourage you to do is to think about what you are trying to achieve by learning Swedish.

You will not learn to speak Swedish so well that in a few short months you are confused for a Swedish native speaker. In fact it is unlikely this will ever happen. Instead of thinking in those kinds of terms, think about, or better yet visualize, what you want to be able to do with the language.

Do you want to get more out of a trip to Sweden? Do you want to communicate better with Swedish family members? Do you want to make an effort to learn the native language of someone you love?

These are all very achievable goals.

I have written this book, not to teach you how to speak fluent Swedish in one week, as that would be impossible anyways, but to give you a shortcut to the Swedish language. This shortcut is achieved by focusing on the areas where Swedish is similar to English and by giving you the rules of Swedish, without getting hung up on the exceptions, so that you can start understanding and speaking Swedish much faster than with traditional methods.

Traditional classroom methods of teaching a foreign language, like the ones you probably remember from school, can be successful with some committed students, but they can take many years to achieve results. Since what is taught in the beginning is often not very useful, if the student does not continue with the course he or she will often remember very little. In contrast to that approach this book will give you an extremely useful introduction to the Swedish language. After completing this book it will be up to you if you continue to learn the language, but even if you go no further than this guide, the basic building blocks of the Swedish language that you will have learned from this book will be useful in the future and bring you closer to your Swedish language goals.

TAKE ADVANTAGE OF ONLINE TOOLS

The internet age has forever changed our approach to language learning. It is now easy, with no more than a quick Google search and a few clicks of the mouse, to listen to Swedish radio, watch a Swedish comedy or read the news in Swedish. In addition to media for native speakers, there is a seemingly never-ending supply of material to learn almost any new language.

Two tools that I recommend to complement this book are:

forvo.com
A language book like this one can be a great introduction to a new language. As adults we crave explanations as to why the language works the way it does and try to find the underlying "rules" or "patterns" and books like this are useful to give these explanations. The major downside to language books of course is that you cannot hear the language spoken. Forvo solves this problem.

Go to forvo.com and type in any Swedish word in this book and immediately hear it pronounced by a native speaker!

<u>Anki</u>
It has been said that repetition is the mother of all learning, and when it comes to learning vocabulary it is hard to argue with this logic. Anki is a spaced-repetition flashcard program that you can install on a computer or as an app on your smartphone or tablet. Make flashcards of the Swedish words you want to memorize and Anki will decide when you need to see that word next in order to efficiently memorize it.

It is my sincere hope that this book proves useful to you and helps you achieve your Swedish language goals.

THE SWEDISH ALPHABET

The Swedish language uses the same Latin alphabet as English, but with the addition of 3 new letters sorted after the z. The letters with their names in Swedish are given in the table below:

Swedish Letter	Swedish Name
a	a
b	be
c	se
d	de
e	e
f	eff
g	ge
h	hå
i	i
j	ji
k	kå
l	ell
m	em
n	en
o	o

Handwritten annotations:

Var = where

a — ar — father
b — b — beer
c — k — kite before a,o,u,å / s — sea elsewhere
d — dog
e — a — café 'a' / bed 'eh'
f — feet
g — g — good a o u å / y — yes after e, i, y, ä, ö
h — his / silent by consonant
i — ee — bee / i — sit
j — y — yes
k — kick / tj — ei y ä ö
l — light
m — meet
n — net
o — oo — food / not short sound not

god "good"
Morgon

HARD vowels a o u å

p	pe	pe
q	ku	like english
r	ärr	rolled
s	ess	sit
t	te	ten
u	u	oo rude / er butcher
v	ve	van
w	dubbel-ve	van
x	eks	taxi
y	y	u cute
z	säta	s set
å *(or)*	å	o more=jag cot (or)
ä *(air)*	ä	ai fair : air
ö *(er)*	ö	ir thirst

jag

Tj
Sj   soft 'sh - lots of air escaping

6

SWEDISH PRONUNCIATION GUIDE

Pronunciation is one of the more difficult aspects of the Swedish language and the relationship between the written word and the spoken word is not always clear. Swedish has silent letters and a few strange sounds that make it difficult to achieve correct pronunciation for an English speaker.

Swedish also possesses tone, or pitch, accent. This feature has disappeared in most other European languages and responsible for the Swedish language's 'singsong rhythm'. This feature is not marked in the written language and must be learned by listening to Swedish speakers. Beginner's should not worry about it however as it is quite difficult and the wrong pitch won't affect you being understood.

Below is a rough guide to reading words in Swedish. Remember that it is common to find words that break these "rules" and spoken Swedish does not always closely follow the written word.

Swedish Letter(s)	Pronunciation Guideline
a	"a" as in father
b	"b" as in beer
c	"k" as in kite before a, o, u or å; "s" as in sea elsewhere
d	"d" as in dog
e	"e" as in cafe or "e" as in bed

f	"**f**" as in **f**eet
g	"**g**" as in **g**ood normally; before e, i, y, ä, or ö: "**y**" as in **y**es; often silent at the end of a word
h	"**h**" as in **h**is; silent before a consonant such as j
i	"**ee**" as in b**ee** or "**i**" as in s**i**t
j	"**y**" as in **y**es
k	"**k**" as in **k**ick normally; before e, i, y, ä, and ö: the "**tj**" sound (see section below)
l	"**l**" as in **l**ight
m	"**m**" as in **m**eat
n	"**n**" as in **n**et
o	"**oo**" as in f**oo**d or "**o**" as in n**o**t
p	"**p**" as in **p**ie
q	similar to English (rarely used)
r	a rolled "**r**" sound like in Spanish
s	always "**s**" as in **s**it; never with a "z" sound like in hou**s**es
t	"**t**" as in **t**en normally; silent when a word ends in et
u	"**u**" as in r**u**de or "**u**" as in b**u**tcher

v	"v" as in van
w	"v" as in van (rarely used)
x	"x" as in taxi
y	"u" as in cute but with lips more rounded. Similar to the French "u" or German "ü"
z	"s" as in set
å	"o" as in more or "o" as in cot
ä	"ai" as in fair or "e" in best
ö	"ir" as in thirst but shorter. Same as the German ö

THE "TJ" SOUND

There are two sounds in Swedish that can be difficult for English speakers to pronounce correctly. One is the "tj" sound. This sound is a soft "sh" sound, but with more air escaping from the mouth creating a softer sound than the English "sh". If you are familiar with German this is the "ch" sound in the German word **ich**. The "tj" sound is spelled "ch", "kj", "tj" or "k" before e, i, y, ä, or ö.

THE "SJ" SOUND

This sound is unique to Swedish and difficult for beginners to pronounce. It is roughly like a strong "h" sound or the German "ch" in **doch** followed by a "w" sound. To get a feel for this word ask a native speaker to pronounce **sked** or go to forvo.com and listen to this word. The "sj" sound is mainly spelled "sj", "sch", "sk" before e, i, y, ä, and ö, "skj" or "stj".

9

SWEDISH–ENGLISH COGNATES

Swedish and English are closely related languages that share a lot of their core vocabulary. This includes:

ANIMALS

katt – cat
fisk – fish
mus – mouse
ko – cow
lamm – lamb

PARTS OF THE BODY

arm – arm
finger – finger
knä – knee
fot – foot
hår – hair

HOUSEHOLD ITEMS

hus – house
rum – room
dörr – door
kniv – knife

FAMILY MEMBERS

moder – mother (usually shortened to **mor**)
fader – father (usually shortened to **far**)
broder – brother (usually shortened to **bror**)
syster – sister
son – son
dotter – daughter

SIMPLE VERBS

dricka – drink
kyssa – kiss
flyga – fly
gå – go
kan – can (be able to)

As an English speaker these cognates are very helpful and make learning the Swedish language much easier than learning an unrelated language. Pay attention to words that are cognates but do not have the exact same meaning in English as in Swedish. For example **hund** in Swedish is "dog" and not just a hunting dog like the English word "hound". There are also some false-cognates (or "false-friends"), i.e. words that look similar but whose meanings are not the same. A famous example is the Swedish word **gift**, which means either "poison" or "married" but never "gift"!

In addition to basic vocabulary, the grammar of Swedish has a lot in common with the grammar of English.

The word order is largely the same:

Du kan dricka kaffe med mjölk.
You can drink coffee with milk.

Kan jag sitta här?
Can I sit here?

There are no case declensions in Swedish except for the genitive (possessive form), which adds an –s ending in a similar way to English.

en flicka
a girl

en flickas hus
a girl's house (no apostrophe in Swedish)

Swedish and English have similar systems of "weak" verbs and "strong" verbs. Like in English, "weak" verbs add a –d or –t sound in the past tense and are considered regular, whereas "strong" verbs change vowel sounds in the past tense and are irregular. For example:

<u>Weak verb</u>
jag dansar – jag dansade – jag har dansat
I dance – I danced – I have danced

<u>Strong verb</u>
vi dricker – vi drack – vi har druckit
we drink – we drank – we have drunk

Change of vowel

The structure of Swedish is in many ways similar to that of English, and this is a real advantage to learning Swedish as an English speaker.

Unfortunately the pronunciation is not as similar as the grammar!

A.

Common	Neuter
en	ett

en pojke	ett hus
en flicka	ett äpple _apple_
en hund	ett djur
en katt	
en fisk	
en ko	
en gris (pig)	
en häst	

The

EN	Et
COMMON	Neuter
pojken	huset
flickan	äpplet

NOUN GENDERS AND PLURALS

GENDER

Like most European languages, but unlike English, Swedish nouns have grammatical gender. Swedish nouns come in one of two genders: common or neuter. The distribution of nouns into genders is essentially arbitrary and the gender of a noun must therefore be memorized alongside the noun. Most living things are common gender in Swedish, although even this rule has exceptions.

The gender of the noun determines the articles that are used with that noun. The word for "a/an" in Swedish changes depending on the gender of the noun, **en** for common gender nouns and **ett** for neuter nouns.

en pojke – en flicka
a boy – a girl

ett hus – ett äpple
a house – an apple

The word for "the" in Swedish actually attaches to the end of the word as a suffix. For common nouns this form is **–en** and for neuter nouns it is **–et**. Note that if the word ends in an **–a** or **–e**, then only **–n** or **–t** is added to the end of the word and the vowels are not doubled.

pojken – flickan
the boy – the girl

huset – äpplet
the house – the apple

PLURALS

Forming plurals in Swedish is more complicated than English; there are several different plural suffixes, none of which is the **–s** ending like in English. For **–en** words, the two main plural suffixes are: **–ar** and **–or**. The main rule is that **–en** words that end in a consonant or an **–e**, add **–ar** in the plural, and **–en** words that end in **–a**, add **–or**. In both cases you remove the end vowel first and never double the vowels.

en pojke – pojkar
a boy – boys

en flicka – flickor
a girl – girls

For **–et** words the two main plural suffixes are **–n** and no ending. The rule is that **–et** words that end in a vowel add **–n**, and **–et** words that end in a consonant do not add an ending, which makes them the same in the singular and plural.

ett äpple – äpplen
an apple – apples

ett hus – hus
a house – houses

Note that it is important to know if a noun is common gender (**–en** word) or neuter gender (**–et** word) because if you mistake **äpple** for an **–en** word, then you would think **äpplen** means "the apple" when in fact it means "apples".

Apart from the four endings above, there are numerous exceptions in Swedish. One exception is that some nouns, especially foreign borrowings, add **–er** to form the plural.

en telefon – telefoner
a telephone – telephones

There are also irregular nouns in Swedish that do not follow any pattern when forming the plural form. This is similar to the situation in English with words like child – children, foot – feet, tooth – teeth etc. These nouns must therefore be memorized as there is no shortcut way to figure them out.

Like in the singular, to say "the boys", we add an ending to the plural form of the word. This form, called the plural definite form, adds –na to the plural for most nouns. If the plural form already ends in an –n, then only –a is added.

en pojke – pojken – pojkar – pojkarna
a boy – the boy – boys – the boys

en flicka – flickan – flickor – flickorna
a girl – the girl – girls – the girls

ett äpple – äpplet – äpplen – äpplena
an apple – the apple – apples – the apples

Neuter nouns (–et words) that end in a consonant and do not add an ending to form the plural, add –en to form the plural definite.

ett hus – huset – hus – husen
a house – the house – houses – the houses

Many irregular plural nouns which do not have –r or –n endings in the plural form, also add –en to form the plural definite form.

en mus – musen – möss – mössen
a mouse – the mouse – mice – the mice

Notice this Swedish irregular noun is also irregular in English. Because Swedish and English are related languages this will often be the case.

PLURALS

COMMON NOUNS = EN

They end in our e ~ pojke ⟶ pojkar

if they end in a become or e
        eg flicka ⟶ flickor

NEUTER NOUNS = Ett

äpple ⟶ add N = applen

hus ⟶ same = hus

Nouns of foreign origin often add er

en telefon
    telefoner

COMMON SWEDISH NOUNS

Below is a list of common Swedish nouns. The plural form is given in parentheses. Note that some nouns do not have a plural form in Swedish.

ANIMALS

ett djur (djur) – an animal (animals)
en hund (hundar) – a dog (dogs)
en katt (katter) – a cat (cats)
en fisk (fiskar) – a fish (fish)
en fågel (fåglar) – a bird (birds)
en ko (kor) – a cow (cows)
en gris (grisar) – a pig (pig)
en mus (möss) – a mouse (mice)
en häst (hästar) – a horse (horses)

PEOPLE

en person (personer) – a person (people)
en mor (mödrar) – a mother (mothers)
en far (fäder) – a father (fathers)
en son (söner) – a son (sons)
en dotter (döttrar) – a daughter (daughters)
en bror (brödre) – a brother (brothers)
en syster (systrar) – a sister (sisters)
en man (män) – a man (men)
en kvinna (kvinnor) – a woman (women)
en pojke (pojkar) – a boy (boys)
en flicka (flickor) – a girl (girls)
ett barn (barn) – a child (children)
en vän (vänner) – a friend (friends)

19

PARTS OF THE BODY

en kropp (kroppar) – a body (bodies)
ett huvud (huvuden) – a head (heads)
ett ansikte (ansikten) – a face (faces)
ett hår (hår) – a hair (hairs)
ett öga (ögon) – an eye (eyes)
en mun (munnar) – a mouth (mouths)
en näse (näsor) – a nose (noses)
ett öra (öran) – an ear (ears)
en hand (händer) – a hand (hands)
en arm (armar) – an arm (arms)
en fot (fötter) – a foot (feet)
ett ben (ben) – a leg (legs)
ett hjärta (hjärtan) – a heart (hearts)
ett blod – blood
ett ben (ben) – a bone (bones)
ett skägg (skägg) – a beard (beards)

FOOD & DRINK

en mat – food
ett kött – meat
ett bröd (bröd) – bread (breads)
en ost (ostar) – cheese (cheeses)
ett äpple (äpplen) – apple (apples)
ett vatten – water
en öl (öl) – beer
en vin (viner) – wine (wines)
ett kaffe – coffee
ett te – tea
en mjölk – milk

PRONOUNS

The system of pronouns in Swedish is very similar to English. The subject pronouns are:

jag – I
du – you
han – he
hon – she
den / det – it   (den = en wird   det = ett word)
vi – we
ni – you (polite or plural)
de – they (**de** is pronounced "dom")

Note that there are two forms for "it"; **den** is used when referring to –**en** words and **det** when referring to –**et** words. Also note the Swedish word **ni** is used to be more polite or formal to a single person or to address more than one person. This is similar to use of vous in French.

Just like in English, Swedish has a different set of object pronouns (the difference between "I" and "me" in English). The object pronouns are:

mig – me (**mig** sounds like "may")
dig – you (**dig** sounds like "day")
honom – him
henne – her
den / det – it
oss – us
er – you (polite or plural)
dem – them

Jag älskar dig ~~day~~ → object pronouns
I love you

Du älskar mig ~~may~~
You love me

Han älskar henne
He loves her

Hon älskar honom
She loves him

Swedish also has a set of possessive pronouns that correspond to the English "my", "your" etc. The possessive pronouns are:

min / mitt / mina – my / mine
din / ditt / dina – your / yours
hans – his
hennes – her
dess – its
vår / vårt / våra – our / ours
er / ert / era – your (plural) / yours (plural)
deras – their / theirs

The forms for "my", "your" and "our" change form depending on the gender and number of the noun that is owned.

min arm
my arm (**–en** word)

mitt hår
my hair (**–et** word)

dina hästar
your horses (plural)

The possessive pronouns in Swedish are used for both the possessive pronouns and the possessive adjectives, meaning that the same word is used for the English "my" and "mine".

min hund
my dog

hunden är min
the dog is mine

mina hundar
my dogs

hundarna är mina
the dogs are mine

SWEDISH VERBS:
PRESENT AND PAST TENSES

PRESENT TENSE

This is where Swedish gets easy!

Conjugating verbs is one way where Swedish is simpler than most European languages including English. In Swedish, verbs do not change form for person or number, meaning that in any given tense there is only a single form of the verb and there are no exceptions.

To illustrate this let's look at three verbs: "to be", "to have" and "to love". Notice that there are various different forms in English, but there is only a single form in Swedish:

> **jag är** – I am
> **du är** – you are
> **hon är** – she is
> **vi är** – we are
> **ni är** – you are
> *dom* **de är** – they are

> **jag har** – I have
> **du har** – you have
> **hon har** – she has
> **vi har** – we have
> **ni har** – you have
> **de har** – they have

jag älskar – I love
du älskar – you love
han älskar – he loves
vi älskar – we love
ni älskar – you love
de älskar – they love

As you can see this is simpler than English and much simpler than languages like Spanish and Italian that have a different form for each person.

To negate verbs you simply add **inte** after the verb that you want to negate:

han älskar inte
he does not love

PAST TENSE

Just like English, Swedish verbs have two different past tense forms, called "weak verbs" and "strong verbs". The weak verbs, also called "regular verbs", in English are verbs that simply add a – d or –ed ending to form the past tense, such as walk – walked, admire – admired, escape – escaped etc.

The most common type of weak verb in Swedish adds –**de** to the basic form of the verb to make the past tense. As in the present tense, the same form of the verb is used regardless of person.

jag arbetar – jag arbetade
I work – I worked

du hoppar – du hoppade
you jump – you jumped

Some weak verbs in Swedish add –te to the stem of the verb instead of –de to form the past tense.

de leker – de lekte
they play – they played

vi kysser – vi kysste
we kiss – we kissed

Swedish strong verbs involve a vowel change to the stem in order to form the past tense. This corresponds to English irregular verbs such as drink – drank, run – ran, fly – flew. Like in English the strong verbs in Swedish are irregular and there is no general rule that can be learned as a shortcut. The number of Swedish strong verbs is relatively small, but many are basic common words. Many verbs that are irregular in English are also irregular in Swedish, such as:

jag säger
I say

du sade
you said

hon gå
she goes

han gick
he went

ni dricker
you drink

de drack
they drank

COMMON SWEDISH VERBS

Below is a list of common verbs in Swedish, listed with the infinitive, the present tense form and the past tense form. Note that many common verbs are similar to English.

Infin *Pres* *Past*

vara – är – var – to be
ha – har – hade – to have
göra – gör – gjorde – to do
säga – säger – sade – to say
tala – talar – talade – to speak
se – ser – såg – to see
gå – går – gick – to go / walk
springa – springer – sprang – to run
hoppa – hoppar – hoppade – to jump
arbeta – arbetar – arbetade – to work
leka – leker – lekte – to play
flyga – flyger - flög – to fly
simma – simmer – simmade – to swim
äta – äter – åt – to eat
dricka – dricker – drack – to drink
laga – lagar – lagade – to cook
skratta – skrattar – skrattade – to laugh
gråta – gråter – grät – to cry
sitta – sitter – satt – to sit
stå – står – stod – to stand
älska – älskar – älskade – to love
hata – hatar – hatade – to hate
kyssa – kysser – kysste – to kiss
dansa – dansar – dansade – to dance
sova – sover – sov – to sleep
sjunga – sjunger – sjöng – to sing
lära – lär – lärde – to learn
tänka – tänker – tankte – to think

29

läsa – läser – läste – to read
skriva – skriver – skrev – to write
öppna – öppnar – öppnade – to open
stänga – stänger – stängde – to close
köpa – köper – köpte – to buy
betala – betalar – betalade – to pay
sälja – säljer – sålde – to sell

ADJECTIVES

Adjectives in Swedish inflect for gender and number.

As we have already seen, when you want to say "the dog" or "the house", the definite article is added to the end of the word.

hunden
the dog

huset
the house

hundarna
the dogs

If you want to add an adjective to this phrase and say "the big dog" or "the big house", a different form of "the" is also added before the adjective. This form depends on the gender and number of the noun, **den** for –en words, **det** for –et words and **de** for all plurals regardless of gender.

den stora hunden
the big dog

det stora huset
the big house

de stora hundarna
the big dogs

The word for "big" in Swedish is **stor**, however between "the" and the noun an **–a** is added in each case to make **stora**. Note that in English this would literally be "the big the dog" which makes no sense, but this is the correct way to say this in Swedish.

If instead you want to say "a big dog" or "a big house", in Swedish there are three different forms of the adjective depending again on the gender and number of the noun. The three forms are as follows:

en stor hund
a big dog

ett stort hus
a big house

stora hundar
big dogs

The three forms of the adjective are: no ending for **–en** nouns, **–t** for **–et** nouns and **–a** for all plural nouns regardless of gender. The same three forms are used if instead of "a big dog" you want to say "the dog is big".

hunden är stor
the dog is big

huset är stort
the house is big

hundarna är stora
the dogs are big

This is the basic pattern in Swedish for all adjectives; however there are a few exceptions that have to be learned on a case by case basis.

SWEDISH NUMBERS, DAYS AND MONTHS

NUMBERS

ett – one
två – two
tre – three
fyra – four
fem – five
sex – six
sju – seven
åtta – eight
nio – nine
tio – ten
elva – eleven
tolv – twelve
tretton – thirteen
fjorton – fourteen
femton – fifteen
sexton – sixteen
sjutton – seventeen
arton – eighteen
nitton – nineteen
tjugo – twenty
trettio – thirty
fyrtio – forty
femtio – fifty
sextio – sixty
sjuttio – seventy
åttio – eighty
nittio – ninety
ett hundra – one hundred
ett tusen – one thousand

DAYS OF THE WEEK

måndag – Monday
tisdag – Tuesday
onsdag – Wednesday
torsdag – Thursday
fredag – Friday
lördag – Saturday
söndag – Sunday

MONTHS OF THE YEAR

januari – January
februari – February
mars – March
april – April
maj – May
juni – June
juli – July
augusti – August
september – September
oktober – October
november – November
december – December

Seasons
vinter (vintern) → winter
var (varen) → spring

USEFUL SWEDISH PHRASES

Hej
Hi

Hur står det till? *Hur nar du*
How are you?

Bara bra, tack. *jag na bra tack*
Just fine, thank you

Ja
Yes

Nej
No

Vad heter du?
What is your name?

Jag heter Sven.
My name is Sven.

Nice / glad
Trevligt att träffas.
Nice to meet you.

Var kommer du ifrån??
Where are you from?

Jag kommer från Sverige.
I am from Sweden

God morgon
Good morning

God eftermiddag
Good afternoon

God kväll
Good evening

God natt
Good night

Hej då
Good bye

Ursäkta
Excuse me

Snälla
Please

Tack
Thank you

Jag förstår inte
I don't understand

Jag vet inte
I don't know

Snakker du engelsk?
Do you speak English?

Talar du svenska?
Do you speak Swedish?

Ja, lite.
Yes, a little.

Jag talar väldigt lite svenska
I only speak very little Swedish

GLOSSARY – THEMATIC ORDER

ANIMALS

djur (–et, –)	animal
hund (–en, –ar)	dog
katt (–en, –er)	cat
fisk (–en, –ar)	fish
fågel (–n, fåglar)	bird
ko (–n, –r)	cow
gris (–en, –ar)	pig
mus (–en, möss)	mouse
häst (–en, –ar)	horse

PEOPLE

person (–en, –er)	person
mor (modern, mödrar)	mother
far (fadern, fäder)	father
son (–en, söner)	son
dotter (–n, döttrar)	daughter
bror (brodern, bröder)	brother
syster (–n, systrar)	sister
vän (–nen, –ner)	friend
man (–nen, män)	man
kvinna (–n, –or)	woman
pojke (–n, –ar)	boy
flicka (–n, –or)	girl
barn (–et, –)	child

LOCATION

stad (–en, städer)	city
hus (–et, –)	house
gata (–n, –or)	street
flygplats (–en, –er)	airport
hotell (–et, –er)	hotel
restaurang (–en, –er)	restaurant
skola (–n, –or)	school
universitet (–et, –)	university
park (–en, –er)	park
butik (–en, –er)	store / shop
sjukhus (–et, –)	hospital
kyrka (–n, –or)	church
land (–et, länder)	country (state)
bank (–en, –er)	bank
marknad (–en, –er)	market

HOME

bord (–et, –)	table
stol (–en, –ar)	chair
fönster (fönstret, –)	window
dörr (–en, –ar)	door
bok (–en, böcker)	book

CLOTHING

kläder (–na)	clothing
hatt (–en, –ar)	hat
klänning (–en, –ar)	dress
skjorta (–n, –or)	shirt
byxa (–n, –or)	pants
sko (–n, –or)	shoe

BODY

kropp (–en, –ar)	body
huvud (–et, –en)	head
ansikte (–et, –en)	face
hår (–et, –)	hair
öga (–t, ögon)	eye
mun (–nen, –nar)	mouth
näsa (–n, –or)	nose
öra (–t, –n)	ear
hand (–en, händer)	hand
arm (–en, –ar)	arm
fot (–en, fötter)	foot
ben (–et, –)	leg
hjärta (–t, –n)	heart
blod (–et)	blood
ben (–et, –)	bone
skägg (–et, –)	beard

MISCELLANEOUS

ja	yes
nej	no

FOOD & DRINK

ägg (et)

mat (–en)	*egg* food
kött (–et)	meat
bröd (–et, –)	bread
ost (–en, –ar)	cheese
äpple (–et, –en)	apple
vatten (vattnet, –)	water
öl (–en, –)	beer
vin (–en, –er)	wine
kaffe (–t)	coffee
te (–et, –er)	tea
mjölk (–en)	milk

soppa (an)   *soup*

salt (et)   *salt*

frukost (–en, –ar)	breakfast
lunch (–en, –er)	lunch
middag (–en, –ar)	dinner

COLORS

färg (–n, –r)	color
röd (rött, –a)	red
blå (–tt, –a)	blue
grön (–t, –a)	green
gul (–t, –a)	yellow
svart (–, –a)	black
vit (–t, –a)	white

NATURE

hav (–et, –)	sea
flod (–en, –er)	river
sjö (–n, –ar)	lake
berg (–et, –)	mountain
regn (–et)	rain
snö (–n)	snow
träd (–et, –)	tree
blomma (–n, –or)	flower
sol (–en, –ar)	sun
måne (–n, –ar)	moon
vind (–en, –ar)	wind
himmel (himlen, himlar)	sky
eld (–en, –ar)	fire
is (–en, –ar)	ice
hav (–et, –)	sea

COMMON VERBS

vara (är, var)	be
ha (har, hade)	have
göra (gör, gjorde)	do
säga (–er, sade)	say
tala (–r, –de)	speak
se (–r, såg)	see
gå (–r, gick)	go / walk
springa (–er, sprang)	run
hoppa (–r, –de)	jump
arbeta (–r, –de)	work
leka (–er, lekte)	play
flyga (–er, flög)	fly
simma (–r, –de)	swim
äta (–r, åt)	eat
dricka (–er, drack)	drink
laga (–r, –de)	cook
skratta (–r, –de)	laugh
gråta (–er, grät)	cry
sitta (–er, satt)	sit
stå (–r, stod)	stand
älska(–r, –de)	love
hata(–r, –de)	hate
kyssa (–er, kysste)	kiss
dansa (–r, –de)	dance
sova (–er, sov)	sleep
sjunga (–er, sjöng)	sing
lära (lär, lärde)	learn
tänka (–er, tankte)	think
läsa (–er, läste)	read
skriva (–er, skrev)	write
öppna (–r, –de)	open
stänga (–er, stängde)	close
köpa (–er, köpte)	buy
betala (–r, –de)	pay
sälja (–er, sålde)	sell

ADJECTIVES

stor (–t, –a)	big
liten (litet, små)	small
god (gott, –a)	good
dålig (–t, –a)	bad
het (–t, –a)	hot
kall (–t, –a)	cold
billig (–t, –a)	cheap
dyr (–t, –a)	expensive
glad (glatt, –a)	happy
ledsen (ledset, ledsna)	sad
stor (–t, –e)	big

TIME

dag (–en, –ar)	day
månad (–en, –er)	month
år (–et, –)	year
timme (–n, –ar)	hour
i dag	today
i morgon	tomorrow
i går	yesterday

SEASONS

sommar (–en, somrar)	summer
höst (–en, –ar)	fall
vinter (–n, vintrar)	winter
vår (–en, –ar)	spring

GLOSSARY – ALPHABETICAL ORDER

A

ansikte (–et, –en)	face
april	April
arbeta (–r, –de)	work
arm (–en, –ar)	arm
arton	eighteen
augusti	August

anka   *duck*

äpple(n)(en)   *the orange*

ägg(et)   *Egg*

B

bank (–en, –er)	bank
barn (–et, –)	child
ben (–et, –)	leg
ben (–et, –)	bone
berg (–et, –)	mountain
betala (–r, –de)	pay
billig (–t, –a)	cheap
blod (–et)	blood
blomma (–n, –or)	flower
blå (–tt, –a)	blue
bok (–en, böcker)	book
bord (–et, –)	table
bror (brodern, bröder)	brother
bröd (–et, –)	bread
butik (–en, –er)	store / shop
byxa (–n, –or)	pants

D

dag (–en, –ar)	day
dansa (–r, –de)	dance
december	December
djur (–et, –)	animal
dotter (–n, döttrar)	daughter
dricka (–er, drack)	drink
dyr (–t, –a)	expensive
dålig (–t, –a)	bad
dörr (–en, –ar)	door

E

eld (–en, –ar)	fire
elva	eleven
ett	one

engilska   *engwör*

F

far (fadern, fäder)	father
februari	February
fem	five
femtio	fifty
femton	fifteen
fisk (–en, –ar)	fish
fjorton	fourteen
flicka (–n, –or)	girl
flod (–en, –er)	river
flyga (–er, flög)	fly
flygplats (–en, –er)	airport
fot (–en, fötter)	foot
fredag	Friday
frukost (–en, –ar)	breakfast
fyra	four
fyrtio	forty
fågel (–n, fåglar)	bird

fläskkott   *pork*

Frukt (en)   *fruit*

färg (–n, –r)	color
fönster (fönstret, –)	window

G

gata (–n, –or)	street
glad (glatt, –a)	happy
god (gott, –a)	good
gris (–en, –ar)	pig
gråta (–er, grät)	cry
grön (–t, –a)	green
gul (–t, –a)	yellow
gå (–r, gick)	go / walk
göra (gör, gjorde)	do

H

ha (har, hade)	have
hand (–en, händer)	hand
hata(–r, –de)	hate
hatt (–en, –ar)	hat
hav (–et, –)	sea
het (–t, –a)	hot
himmel (himlen, himlar)	sky
hjärta (–t, –n)	heart
hoppa (–r, –de)	jump
hotell (–et, –er)	hotel
hund (–en, –ar)	dog
hundra	hundred
hus (–et, –)	house
huvud (–et, –en)	head
hår (–et, –)	hair
häst (–en, –ar)	horse
höst (–en, –ar)	fall (autumn)

I

i dag	today
i går	yesterday
i morgon	tomorrow
is (–en, –ar)	ice

inte — *nor (after the verb)*

J

ja	yes
januari	January
juli	July
juni	June

jordgubbe(n)

K

kaffe (–t)	coffee
kall (–t, –a)	cold
katt (–en, –er)	cat
kläder (–na)	clothing
klänning (–en, –ar)	dress
ko (–n, –r)	cow
köpa (–er, köpte)	buy
kött (–et)	meat
kropp (–en, –ar)	body
kvinna (–n, –or)	woman
kyrka (–n, –or)	church
kyssa (–er, kysste)	kiss

kyckling(en) — *chicken (shicklagen)*

L

laga (–r, –de)	cook
land (–et, länder)	country (state)
ledsen (ledset, ledsna)	sad
leka (–er, lekte)	play
liten (litet, små)	small
lära (lär, lärde)	learn
läsa (–er, läste)	read
lördag	Saturday
lunch (–en, –er)	lunch

M

maj	May
man (–nen, män)	man
marknad (–en, –er)	market
mars	March
mat (–en)	food
middag (–en, –ar)	dinner
mjölk (–en)	milk
mor (modern, mödrar)	mother
mun (–nen, –nar)	mouth
mus (–en, möss)	mouse
månad (–en, –er)	month
måndag	Monday
måne (–n, –ar)	moon

N

nej	no
nio	nine
nittio	ninety
nitton	nineteen
november	November
näsa (–n, –or)	nose

nötkött) beef

47

O

oktober	October
onsdag	Wednesday
ost (–en, –ar)	cheese

öl (et) *beer*

P

park (–en, –er)	park
person (–en, –er)	person
pojke (–n, –ar)	boy

pastan (pasta) *pepparn pepper*

R

regn (–et)	rain
restaurang (–en, –er)	restaurant
röd (rött, –a)	red

S

se (–r, såg)	see
september	September
sex	six
sextio	sixty
sexton	sixteen
simma (–r, –de)	swim
sitta (–er, satt)	sit
sju	seven
sjukhus (–et, –)	hospital
sjunga (–er, sjöng)	sing
sjuttio	seventy
sjutton	seventeen
sjö (–n, –ar)	lake
skjorta (–n, –or)	shirt
sko (–n, –or)	shoe
skola (–n, –or)	school

sockret *the sugar*
saltet *the salt*

skratta (–r, –de)	laugh
skriva (–er, skrev)	write
skägg (–et, –)	beard
snö (–n)	snow
sol (–en, –ar)	sun
sommar (–en, somrar)	summer
son (–en, söner)	son
sova (–er, sov)	sleep
springa (–er, sprang)	run
stad (–en, städer)	city
stol (–en, –ar)	chair
stor (–t, –a)	big
stå (–r, stod)	stand
stänga (–er, stängde)	close
svart (–, –a)	black
syster (–n, systrar)	sister
säga (–er, sade)	say
sälja (–er, sålde)	sell
söndag	Sunday

(handwritten: Suorgas (en) Sandwich)

T

tala (–r, –de)	speak
te (–et, –er)	tea
timme (–n, –ar)	hour
tio	ten
tisdag	Tuesday
tjugo	twenty
tolv	twelve
torsdag	Thursday
tre	three
trettio	thirty
tretton	thirteen
träd (–et, –)	tree
tusen	thousand
två	two
tänka (–er, tankte)	think

(handwritten: tomat (er))

49

U

universitet (–et, –)	university

V

vara (är, var)	be
vatten (vattnet, –)	water
vin (–en, –er)	wine
vind (–en, –ar)	wind
vinter (–n, vintrar)	winter
vit (–t, –a)	white
vår (–en, –ar)	spring
vän (–nen, –ner)	friend

vinet
vegeterianen) *Wine*
vegetarian

Å

år (–et, –)	year
åtta	eight
åttio	eighty

Ä

älska(–r, –de)	love
äpple (–et, –en)	apple
äta (–r, åt)	eat

atee
jag ater

Ö

öga (–t, ögon)	eye
öl (–en, –)	beer
öppna (–r, –de)	open
öra (–t, –n)	ear

(irja?)